The Amazing Book of Movie Trivia

Jack Goldstein

THE FACTS

Film Titles

- It was only after Paul Newman was cast in the role of Butch for the film *The Sundance Kid and Butch Cassidy* that the order of characters in the title was changed (obviously to *Butch Cassidy and the Sundance Kid*).

- The original title of *Scream* was *Scary Movie*.

- Like many films, *Airplane!* has different titles in different countries. In Brazil it is called *Tighten Up Your Seatbelt, The Pilot's Gone!*, whereas in Germany it is *The Incredible Trip on a Crazy Airplane*.

- In China, *Final Destination* is called *The Death God Comes*.

- Paramount Pictures insisted that quote marks be put around the crocodile in *"Crocodile" Dundee*, so that potential audiences would not think the main character was an actual crocodile.

- The original title of *Honey, I Shrunk the Kids* was *Teenie Weenies*.

- In Brazil, distributors tried to capitalize on the success of *Back to the Future* by naming Michael J Fox's next movie (which we know as *Teen Wolf*) *Boy From the Future*.

- The working title for E.T. was actually *A Boy's Life*.

- *Ghostbusters* was allegedly originally going to be called *Ghost Smashers*.

- *Halloween* was originally called *The Babysitter Murders*.

Star Wars

- *Star Wars* was in fact originally called *The Star Wars*
- In *The Empire Strikes Back*, if you look carefully, you'll see both a potato and a shoe fly past the camera in the asteroid scene.
- If Carrie Fisher hadn't been available, George Lucas had Jodie Foster down as second choice for the role of Princess Leia.
- Episode II had a rather tongue-in-cheek working title – *Jar Jar's Big Adventure.*
- Darth Vader only has twelve minutes on screen during the first Star Wars Film (*A New Hope*). Despite this, most people would say he is the character that made the biggest impression on them.
- Alec Guinness absolutely hated *Star Wars*, saying that the dialogue was 'a load of rubbish'. He even once said that killing off Obi Wan Kenobi was his idea.
- Vader is actually the Dutch word for 'father'.
- Every single clone trooper featured in *Attack of the Clones* and *Revenge of the Sith* is CGI.
- James Earl Jones (who voices Darth Vader) was so convinced the film would be a flop that he initially refused to allow his name to be used in the credits.
- In the original script for *The Star Wars*, Luke Starkiller (yes) punches fourteen-year-old Princess Leia in the face.

Cameos

- Tim Burton – whose films often have a rather dark and macabre feel – appears as a corpse in Danny DeVito's 1992 film *Hoffa*.

- In *Catch Me If You Can*, the French policeman who arrests Leonardo DiCaprio is in fact the real Frank Abagnale Jr.

- Stan Lee – creator of some of the greatest comic book characters of all time – has a cameo in every film that stars one of his creations.

- Alfred Hitchcock is famous for having cameo roles in his own films; it can be quite fun to try and spot his often not-so-subtle appearances whilst watching one of his masterpieces.

- Ron Jeremy appears in *Ghostbusters*, in the scene where the containment unit explodes.

- Cate Blanchett is the actress who plays Nicholas Angel's girlfriend in *Hot Fuzz* – although as she is only shown wearing a lab-suit, face mask and goggles, you'd be pretty hard-pressed to figure out it was her!

- Also, at the beginning of *Hot Fuzz*, we see a flashback in which Nicholas Angel is stabbed in the hand by a crazed Santa. The man behind the beard? Renowned director Peter Jackson.

- In perhaps one of the hardest-to-spot cameos, Glenn Close plays a bushy-bearded pirate in *Hook* – it's not that the cameo is brief, rather that the make-up is so good you would never guess who is behind it!

- At the time of writing, the *Saw* franchise is the most successful horror series, grossing almost $1 billion worldwide.
- Although it is considered to be one of the greatest films ever, *The Shawshank Redemption* was only the 51st highest grossing film of its year, well behind flicks such as the critically-panned *Street Fighter*.

General Facts

- At the time of writing (and according to IMDB) the worst ever film is 1985 flick *Final Justice*.

- Whilst filming *Schindler's List*, Steven Spielberg regularly got Robin Williams to call the crew and tell jokes to cheer them up. Williams was filming the part of the Genie from *Aladdin* at the time, and some of the jokes he told made it into the movie (obviously *Aladdin*, not *Schindler's List*...)

- Courtney Love has claimed that her ex-boyfriend Kurt Cobain was originally offered the role of Lance, the drug dealer in *Pulp Fiction*; Quentin Tarantino has denied this.

- All three lead actresses from 1976's *Carrie* went on to marry directors – Sissy Spacek married Jack Fisk, Amy Irving married Steven Spielberg, and Nancy Allen tied the knot with Brian De Palma.

- All of the characters in Disney's *Hercules* have Greek names. Except for Hercules that is – his name is Roman. The Greek version of his name is in fact Heracles, however Disney felt this didn't sound quite as good!

- The last mainstream movie released on laserdisc was *End of Days*.

- The filming style of the 2005 version of *War of the Worlds* (where almost everything is filmed from ground level) was influenced by amateur footage of the 9/11 terrorist attacks.

- The HMS Interceptor from *Pirates of the Caribbean* is also the ship used in *Star Trek: Generations*.
- The first animated film to be nominated for best picture Oscar was Disney's 1991 classic *Beauty and the Beast*.
- Bollywood produces twice as many films every year as Hollywood does.

Props – Part 1

- Chocolate syrup was used as the blood in the shower scene from *Psycho* – because the film is in black and white, the colour difference wasn't a problem!

- In the book, the famous Ruby slippers from *The Wizard of Oz* are in fact silver.

- One pair of the slippers (of which there are thought to be four) from the film raised $666,000 at auction in 2000.

- James Cameron drew the charcoal picture of a nude Kate Winslet featured in *Titanic*.

- In *Rocky*, the lead character points out a mistake on a banner at the match venue. This line wasn't scripted; Sly had to do this as the art department had made a genuine mistake!

- The design of the carpet in Sid's hallway in *Toy Story* is almost identical to one of the hotel corridor carpets in The Shining.

- The mask used by Michael Myers in *Halloween* was a Captain Kirk mask painted white.

- The faeces used in the iconic toilet scene in *Trainspotting* was actually made out of chocolate, and apparently smelt delicious.

- A real horse's head (purchased from a local dog-food factory) was used for the iconic scene in *The Godfather*. John Marley wasn't told that the plastic prop that they had been using had been replaced, and therefore his reaction is real!
- In *Highlander*, the swords were made to spark by wires which ran down the actors' sleeves and were connected to car batteries. Dangerous, anyone...?

Cast – Part 1

- Barbie in *Toy Story* and Ariel in *The Little Mermaid* are voiced by the same actress, Jodi Benson.

- In *Home Alone,* the photo of Buzz's girlfriend is actually a boy – the director thought it would be too cruel to choose an ugly girl for the humorous purpose.

- Peter Ostrum who played Charlie in *Willy Wonka and the Chocolate Factory* never acted in another film and actually went on to become a vet.

- Bela Lugosi was the actor responsible for the most iconic portrayal of Dracula on film. When he died, he was actually buried in costume.

- Disney wanted the Beatles to voice the vultures in *The Jungle Book,* however killjoy John Lennon stopped it from happening.

- Tom Cruise was offered the role of *Edward Scissorhands*, but thought the movie was a bit weird for his liking.

- Each actor who portrayed a member of the wolf pack in *The Twilight Saga: New Moon* had to show documentation to prove they were of Native American descent.

- The largest non-human cast ever featured in a film was for Irwin Allen's 1978 movie *The Swarm*, in which 22 million bees were used.

- Jack Nicholson was considered for the role of Hannibal Lecter in *Silence of the Lambs*.

▶ Stanley Kubrick put a great deal of thought into who to cast as Jack in *The Shining*. He first considered Robert De Niro, but after watching *Taxi Driver*, he didn't think he was psychotic enough. He then thought about Robin Williams, but having watched *Mork and Mindy*, Kubrick thought he came across as a little *too* psychotic. In the end, he cast Jack Nicholson, who displayed just the right amount of madness...

Surprising Facts

- The idea for the poster of *The Usual Suspects* came before a single word of the script was written.

- When John Lasseter, Pete Docter and Joe Ranft had lunch together at Pixar in 1994, in that single meeting alone they came up with the ideas for *A Bug's Life*, *Monsters Inc*, *Finding Nemo* and *Wall-E*.

- Sigourney Weaver actually pulled off the basketball shot in *Alien: Resurrection* for real.

- Sean Connery played Indiana Jones's father in *The Last Crusade* – even though there's only 12 years between the two actors!

- *Psycho* was the first film in America to show a toilet flushing.

- The police sirens you hear during the casino scene in *Swingers* were real – it was the police on their way to stop the filming, as the filmmakers were shooting without a permit.

- The lights over the eggs in *Alien* were actually leant to Ridley Scott by The Who – they were practising their laser show next door to the set.

- In the US, *The Dark Knight* made more money in its first six days than *Batman Begins* made in its entire run.

- Nicolas Winding Refn, the director of *Drive*, failed his driving test eight times.

- The final scene of *Casablanca* was shot on a small sound stage, with the airplane being a cardboard cut-out, and the ground crew played by short people.

Problems, Problems

- The shooting of *No Country for Old Men* was delayed for an entire day when a huge smoke cloud appeared. It was from the set of *There Will Be Blood* which was also filming nearby.

- A number of major scenes in *Braveheart* had to be re-shot when it was noticed that extras were wearing sunglasses and watches!

- There was supposed to be a sequel to *The Breakfast Club*, filmed ten years after the original. It never happened however, as Judd Nelson and John Hughes hated each other.

- During the filming of *The Hunger Games*, Jennifer Lawrence accidentally kicked Josh Hutcherson in the head and knocked him out.

- Dr Seuss's family hated the film adaptation of *The Cat in the Hat* so much that they vowed never to allow another live-action adaptation of any of his books.

- When Walt Disney hired renowned conductor Leopold Stokowski to handle the score for a short he was making called *The Sorcerer's Apprentice*, things went way over budget. Rather than write off the debt however, Disney decided to spend even more money, but make it into a full-length feature – and this is how *Fantasia* came about.

- Whilst filming *Black Swan*, Natalie Portman dislocated a rib. The production budget for the film was so low that they couldn't afford a medic; Natalie gave up her trailer so one could be hired.

- Macaulay Culkin still has a scar on his finger from where Joe Pesci bit him during the filming of *Home Alone*.

- *Charlie and the Great Glass Elevator* was never made into a film because author Roald Dahl hated how *Willy Wonka and the Chocolate Factory* turned out.

- In *Django Unchained*, there is a scene where Leonardo DiCaprio slams his hand onto a table and breaks a glass. This was by accident, and even though he cut his hand open, he carried on filming the scene. The take was used in the final cut.

Amazing Facts

- The first letters of the main characters' names in *Inception* spell 'dreams' – Dom, Robert, Eames, Arthur, Mallorie and Saito.

- *King Kong* was Adolf Hitler's favourite movie.

- Disney were sued by animal activists for their portrayal of Hyenas as evil in *The Lion King*.

- Nicolas Cage was in the frame to play the lead role in *Superman Lives*, a 90s reboot of the franchise directed by Tim Burton. If only it had been made...

- There is a film called *Atuk* which appears to be cursed – every star who has been in the frame for the lead role has tragically died. John Belushi was the original intended for the role, but died of a drug overdose in 1982. Next up, Sam Kinison was killed in a car crash. In 1994 it was offered to John Candy, but he then died of a heart attack. Chris Farley then held talks with producers to take the lead, however he then died of a drug overdose. The script has now been placed 'on hold'.

- Actual veterans of the American Civil War attended the premiere of *Gone with the Wind*.

- Each munchkin from *The Wizard of Oz* was paid $50 a week. Toto, the dog, was paid $125.

- James Cameron has spent more time at the wreck of the Titanic than any individual passenger spent on it.

- Jim Caviezel was actually struck by lightning whilst filming the crucifixion scene for *The Passion of the Christ*.
- Because *Die Hard* was based on a novel which was the sequel to a book that had been made into a film in 1968, the role which eventually went to Bruce Willis contractually had to be offered to the star of the prequel – one Frank Sinatra. As you may have guessed however, being 73 years old at the time, he turned it down.

Did You Know?

- In many scenes during *Moulin Rouge* where Nicole Kidman is filmed from the waist up, she was actually sitting in a wheelchair having suffered a serious injury.
- In the film *Pretty Woman*, when Richard Gere snaps the necklace box shut, making Julia Roberts' character jump a little then laugh, it was totally unscripted and this was Julia's genuine reaction.
- Watching scary movies burns more calories than any other genre.
- There is a sound effect called the 'Wilhelm scream' which has been used in over two hundred movies since its first appearance in 1951.
- The first *Saw* movie only took 18 days to film.
- Shrek was amazingly modelled after a real person – a professional wrestler called Maurice Tillet.
- Pixar's movie *Up* was the first ever animated film to open the prestigious Cannes film festival.
- Every single member of both the cast and crew of *The Thing* (1982) was male.
- The 'Hollywood' sign originally said "Hollywoodland' and cost $21,000.
- In real life, Sissy Spacek (who played Carrie) was voted homecoming queen.

James Bond

- According to the novel *You Only Live Twice*, Bond's parents were Scottish and Swiss, and he grew up in two countries – Germany and France.

- Three quarters of the women James Bond has slept with have tried to kill him.

- The scene in *Goldfinger* where James Bond scuba dives into a compound, then removes his wetsuit to reveal a perfectly dry tuxedo is amazingly based on a real event! MI6 agent Peter Tazelaar scuba-dived into the grounds of a Nazi-controlled casino, removed his wetsuit revealing his dry tuxedo, then rescued two fellow spies who were being held captive by the Nazis.

- In the original novels, James Bond wealds a Beretta 418, however this was changed for the movie *Dr No* when a fan wrote to author Ian Fleming and gave him the opinion that a Beretta was a ladies' gun, and the Walther PPK would be a much more manly replacement.

- *From Russia With Love* was the last film that JFK saw before he was assassinated.

- Sean Connery wore a wig for every one of his performances as James Bond.

- Pierce Brosnan was contractually forbidden from wearing full black-tie dress in any non-James Bond film between 1995 and 2002.

- Liam Neeson was offered the role of James Bond for the 1995 film *Goldeneye*, however he turned it down. Neeson said he didn't want to star in action movies!

- Perhaps the most unusual choice ever to have been considered for the role of James Bond is Welsh singer Tom Jones.

- An ex-US Marine called Johnny Stompanato once stormed onto the set of a Bond movie that Sean Connery was making with his girlfriend, actress Lana Turner. Worried that she was being unfaithful to him (and being slightly deranged and hot-headed), he began waving a gun at some of the actors. Connery quickly disarmed him, picked him up and threw him out the back of the set.

Big Changes

- *Ghostbusters* was originally set in a future where ghosts were rampant, and the busters were every day service personnel just like policemen and firemen.

- OJ Simpson was the original choice for the role of *The Terminator*, however the studio insisted on finding someone else – obviously Arnie in the end – as no-one would believe that OJ was a remorseless killer.

- Ronald Reagan was originally announced as having the lead role in *Casablanca*.

- In the novel *The Shining*, the 'scary' room is number 217. However in the film it is 237. The reason for the change is that the Timberline Lodge Hotel (which is used for the exterior shots of The Overlook) requested it; as they have an actual room 217, they thought no-one would want to stay in it having seen the film!

- Bob Dylan was originally chosen to write the soundtrack for *Toy Story*.

- The original title for *The Lion King* was *King of the Jungle* – until someone pointed out that Lions don't actually live in the jungle...!

- Anthony Burgess originally intended to sell the rights for *A Clockwork Orange* to the Rolling Stones, with Mick Jagger playing Alex, and the rest of the band playing the other Droogs. Then Stanley Kubrick came on board, and things got a little more sensible.

- Pixar wanted to feature GI Joe in *Toy Story*, however Hasbro denied them permission when they found out he was going to be blown up by Sid.
- In early drafts of *Back to the Future*, the time machine was not a DeLorean, but a refrigerator.
- Producers wanted John Travolta to star as Maverick in *Top Gun*, however his asking price was too high for them.

Costumes

- The costumes for wonderfully eerie stop-motion film *Coraline* were all knitted by Althea Crome using miniature needles – some of them took six months to make!

- Jim Carrey found his *Grinch* make-up to be so confining that he received special counselling on torture resistant techniques from a US Navy Seal.

- The Tin Man in *The Wizard of Oz* was originally played by an actor called Buddy Ebsen, however he had to be replaced after being hospitalised – he had an allergic reaction to the aluminium powder in his make-up.

- The make-up budget for *Planet of the Apes* totalled 17% of the entire movie's production cost.

- The wookie costumes in Star Wars are made from 100% human hair.

- In preparation for his role in *X-Men: First Class*, James McAvoy shaved his head. However, it turned out that the director wanted his character to have a full head of hair, and so he had to wear extensions for the first month of shooting.

- Pennywise's hair in *It* was in fact actor Tim Curry's *real* hair.

- Harrison Ford kept himself in such good shape between 1989 and 2008 that his costume measurements for *Indiana Jones and the Kingdom of the Crystal Skull* were exactly the same as they were when he filmed *The Last Crusade* 20 years before!

- The killer's robe in *Scream* was originally intended to be white, but the director changed it because it looked too similar to a Ku Klux Klan outfit.
- Part of the costume worn by *Edward Scissorhands* was made from an old sofa from Tim Burton's first apartment.

Did You Notice?

- The androids in the *Alien* films are named in alphabetical order – Ash, Bishop, Call and David.
- If you speak Norwegian, put your hands over your ears during the opening scene of *The Thing*. The pilots are speaking the language, and give away the entire plot of the film!
- All of the clocks in *Pulp Fiction* are stuck at 4:20.
- David Bowie's face can be seen hidden in the background of several scenes in *Labyrinth*.
- Cameron Diaz is in *Minority Report* – she is one of the subway passengers, and you never even see her full face.
- There's a pet raven in George Bailey's workshop in *It's a Wonderful Life*. The only reason for this is that the Raven was director Frank Capra's 'lucky charm' and in fact featured in every one of his films from 1938 onwards.
- If you look closely, in the Ark's chamber in *Raiders of the Lost Ark*, you can see hieroglyphs of R2D2 and C3PO.
- You can see Pinocchio in the background of the song scene in the Snuggly Duckling in *Tangled*.
- The word 'ewok' is never actually used in any of the *Star Wars* movies.

- The martial art featured in 2010's *The Karate Kid* is actually a form of Kung Fu, not Karate. The studio however used the title to maintain a connection to the earlier films it is loosely based on.

Original Endings

- A scene was filmed for *Doctor Strangelove* where the end of the world was symbolised by a custard pie fight in the war room. It wasn't used however as director Stanley Kubrick felt it was too jovial.

- Sylvester Stallone's original script for *Rocky* ended with his character throwing the fight with Apollo Creed, earning money by taking a dive... which he uses to open up a pet-shop with Adrian.

- The original ending of *Clerks* sees Dante killed by an armed robber.

- Originally, *Thelma and Louise* safely land their car having driven over the cliff. It suffers no damage and they happily make their way into the distance.

- Not only was Julia Roberts' character addicted to drugs in the original draft of *Pretty Woman*, but the film also ended with Richard Gere abandoning her whilst she crouches on the floor in floods of tears.

- In the first audience previews of *Ice Age,* the character of Diego died. However, so many children burst into tears when they found this out that the studio demanded an additional scene in which we find out he survives.

- Thankfully, the original ending for *Terminator 2* didn't make it into the cinema release. In it, we see Sarah Connor as an old lady in the park, with a voiceover saying how "August 29th 1997 came and went, nothing much happened. Michael Jackson turned 40."

- One proposed ending from *Freddy vs. Jason* was that they would destroy each other, and end up in hell together, where Pinhead from *Hellraiser* would appear, saying "Gentlemen, now what seems to be the problem?"
- An early draft of *Return of the Jedi* saw Han Solo die and Luke so troubled by his final encounter with Darth Vader that he quits fighting with the rebels.
- In *Little Shop of Horrors*, a scene where the giant plant eats Seymour and his girlfriend then destroys New York was actually filmed – but audiences didn't like it and so the ending we see now was filmed instead.

Interesting Facts

- Special permission was granted for the makers of *The Da Vinci Code* to film inside the Louvre. However, because it is so valuable, they were not allowed to shine any light on the Mona Lisa, and therefore a duplicate was constructed for the film.

- There have been many film versions of *Zorro*, the first being released as far back as 1920. However, Antonio Banderas is incredibly the first Hispanic actor to have played the lead role.

- There is a Russian live-action version of *The Hobbit* which was released in 1985. If you search, you will find it on YouTube.

- The earliest background designs for *Finding Nemo* were rejected because they looked too realistic – the studio actually had to make them look 'more cartoony'.

- In *Iron Man*, JARVIS stands for 'Just A Rather Very Intelligent System'.

- *Anchorman: The Legend of Ron Burgundy* was inspired by the biography of a real-life journalist, Jessica Savitch.

- The lead characters in *Pulp Fiction* are called Vincent and Jules, whereas the lead characters in *Twins* are called Vincent and Julius. This is surely no coincidence; Danny DeVito was a producer on Pulp Fiction.

- In *Psycho*, the sound of the knife stabbing the female character in the shower was actually made by knifing a melon.

- On average, each frame of the CGI scenes from *Avatar* took 47 hours to render.
- The first three movies released on VHS in America were *M*A*S*H*, *Patton* and *The Sound of Music*. In today's money, they would cost ninety dollars.

Scripts

- To give him inspiration whilst writing *Taxi Driver*, Paul Schrader supposedly kept a loaded gun by his desk. He finished the script in just five days.

- For the film itself, Robert De Niro improvised the famous "You talkin' to me?" scene – the screenplay just says 'Bickle speaks to himself in a mirror'.

- Animated family film *Rio* is amazingly based on a true story; that of Presley, the rare Spix's Macaw.

- In the original script for *Back to the Future*, Marty and Doc Brown run a video pirating operation, selling dodgy movies to Marty's high school colleagues.

- The word 'zombie' is never used in *Night of the Living Dead*.

- Apparently, a basic script exists for a sequel to *E.T.* called *Nocturnal Fears*. In it, we find out that E.T. is actually called Zreck, and another second alien race (who Zreck's race were at war with) would capture and torture Elliot. Please, Steven, never make this film.

- The words 'Elm Street' are never said in the first *Nightmare on Elm Street* film.

- The author with the most number of film adaptations is William Shakespeare, if you also count modern interpretations (e.g. *West Side Story*) and parodies.

- It is hard to think of a Samuel L Jackson character with whom you don't associate the word motherf****r, however he actually started using it to help overcome his stammer.

- *Final Destination* is actually based on a script for an episode of *The X Files* that didn't make it into the TV show.

Props – Part 2

- The fake testicles from *Step Brothers* cost $20,000 to make

- The green sick in *The Exorcist* is Andersen's Pea Soup. The crew initially went with Campbell's soup, but weren't too happy with how it looked.

- Coconuts were used not just for comedy value in *Monty Python and the Holy Grail* – the filmmakers couldn't afford to hire horses.

- Director Sam Raimi has a 'lucky car' which he has used in every one of his films – even his western *The Quick and the Dead*, set before cars were even invented.

- The apple pie in *American Pie* was actually purchased from Costco.

- Some of the props used in the 2005 version of *King Kong* – including spears, a shield and drums – were original props from the 1933 film which Peter Jackson himself actually owned.

- The mechanical shark used in *Jaws* was nicknamed Bruce.

- The cake in the movie *Sixteen Candles* is actually made out of cardboard.

- In one single afternoon, three $300,000 Aston Martins were destroyed whilst filming *Casino Royale*.

- In *The 40 Year Old Virgin*, Steve Carell's character has his chest hair removed. Amazingly, it was NOT a prop – it was his real hair! The scene had to be filmed in one take, and five cameras were set up to capture the action.

Miscellaneous Facts

- *The Girl with the Dragon Tattoo* was filmed in Sweden during the country's coldest winter for over twenty years.

- Both Tom Cruise and Nicolas Cage were considered for the role of *Iron Man* before producers realised Robert Downey Junior would be the perfect fit.

- Over five hundred vehicles were destroyed during the filming of *Transformers: Dark Side of the Moon* – however they cost the film company nothing... they were given away by an insurance company as they had been damaged by a flood.

- James Cameron wanted to release *Avatar* in 1999, however the price of the technology required back then was almost $400 million, and therefore the project was shelved for eight years until it became more cost-effective.

- The Ewoks in *Star Wars* live on Endor... which also happens to be what JRR Tolkien said the Elves call Middle-Earth... *and* is the name of the village King Saul visits in the bible before his final battle with the Philistines.

- The producers of *Meet the Fockers* had to prove to the MPAA that there was a family in America with the surname 'Focker' before they were allowed to use it as the title of their film.

- There is a cup of coffee (usually though not always Starbucks) in every single scene of *Fight Club*.
- Walt Disney refused Alfred Hitchcock permission to film at Disneyland in the 1960s because he thought the film *Psycho* was 'disgusting'.
- Like so many other famous lines in films, in *Titanic* Leonardo DiCaprio ad-libbed "I'm the king of the world!"
- Christopher Lee was the only main actor from the *Lord of the Rings* trilogy to have read the book before filming. He was a big fan of Tolkien's work and originally auditioned for the role of Gandalf.

Academy Awards

- The very first Academy Awards ceremony was held on the 16th of May 1929 at the Hollywood Roosevelt Hotel. It lasted just fifteen minutes.

- In 1999, Michael Jackson bought David Selznick's best picture Oscar for *Gone with the Wind* for over one and a half million dollars.

- The film itself is the longest ever to have won best picture, with a running time of nearly four hours.

- *The Lord of the Rings: The Return of the King* was nominated for eleven academy awards. It won every single one of them.

- Two other films have also won a total of eleven awards: *Titanic* and *Ben Hur*.

- Despite being nominated for an amazing eight Oscars, Peter O'Toole never won a single one.

- In 1973, Tatum O'Neal became the youngest ever Oscar winner at the age of ten.

- On the other hand, the oldest winner was Christopher Plummer who in 2011 won an Oscar for his role in *Beginners* at the grand old age of 82.

- It might not surprise you to learn that the holder of the most nominations (59) and actual wins (26) is Walt Disney himself.

- Winners are forbidden from selling their award statuettes without first offering them back to the academy for a price of one dollar.

Bad Decisions

- Disney were offered the chance to make *Back to the Future*, but they declined, giving the reason that Marty's relationship 'troubles' with his mother could be seen as too controversial for them!

- George Lucas approached Universal Studios with the idea for *Star Wars* in 1973. However, they turned down the then-unknown director.

- When he did get the green light from Fox a few years later however, the studio let him keep the licensing and merchandising rights in exchange for $500,000 less as a director's fee. Latest figures suggest these rights have so far raised $20 billion in sales. Oh well, it probably seemed like a good idea at the time...

- Fox passed up distribution of *The Watchmen* because they thought the script was totally unintelligible.

- Originally, Will Smith was approached to play Neo in *The Matrix*, but backed out at the last minute so he could be in *Wild Wild West*. To be fair however, this hasn't hurt his career as much as it perhaps should have done...

- Robert De Niro turned down the role of Jack Sparrow in *Pirates of the Caribbean* as he thought the film would bomb.

- Miramax turned down the opportunity to make Peter Jackson's *Lord of the Rings* trilogy, as they wanted him to make it into just two films. He went with New Line Cinema in the end, who made $3 billion from the series.

- Before he had even finished filming *On Her Majesty's Secret Service*, George Lazenby decided the James Bond franchise was dead and refused to sign up for any more films as the secret agent. As you can imagine, his career then nosedived.

- Molly Ringwald was a big star in the 80s, but disappeared towards the end of the decade. She was however offered two films in particular, but declined both of them. One was *Ghost*, the other *Pretty Woman*.

- Donald Sutherland chose a $50,000 salary over a 'percentage of profits' deal for his role in *Animal House*. The movie went onto break the box office record for a comedy, meaning Sutherland has lost out on around $20 million.

Family Favourites

- *E.T.* stayed in the US box office top ten for an amazing ten whole months.

- When it was finally released on video, the studio were scared it would be pirated. To combat this, the VHS tapes were made from bright green plastic so people would know the version they bought was genuine.

- Donald Pleasance, who plays Blythe 'The Forger' in *The Great Escape* was in fact the one member of the cast who was a genuine WWII prisoner of war. He had been shot down during a raid over Agenville, and was imprisoned for a year in one of the Stalag Lufts.

- According to Dan Ackroyd, in *Ghostbusters*, Slimer is the ghost of John Belushi.

- Although (or maybe because) he was a life-long fan of *Scooby Doo*, Tim Curry turned down the chance to appear in the live-action movie when he discovered that Scrappy Doo was also going to be in it.

- *Frozen* was the first animated Disney film to have been directed by a woman.

- Rejected names for dwarves in Disney's *Snow White* include Hoppy-Jumpy, Dirty, Gloomy, Gaspy and Shifty.

- 1979's *The Muppet Movie* was cut by the New Zealand censors for featuring 'gratuitous violence'.

- Franz Ferdinand were the original choice for the Weird Sisters at *Harry Potter*'s Yule ball. In the end however, the band was made up of two members of Pulp (Jarvis Cocker and Steve Mackey), two from Radiohead (Jonny Greenwood and Phil Selway), one from All Seeing I (Jason Buckle) and one from Add n to (x) (Steven Claydon).

- JK Rowling told Alan Rickman the secrets of Snape's character years before anyone else knew. He could therefore use the knowledge in his performances throughout the film series. None of the directors were told however, and he was sworn to secrecy – so they had to defer to him on his acting choices.

Stunts

- No CGI was used for the scene in 2002's *Spiderman* where Peter Parker catches Mary Jane's lunch on a tray. The stunt was actually performed by Tobey Maguire, although it did require a number of takes.

- During filming of his 1923 movie *Sherlock, Jr*, Buster Keaton was knocked onto a train track by some rushing water. A decade later, a doctor discovered that Keaton had fractured his neck in the incident!

- When filming the scene in *Die Hard* when Alan Rickman falls from the Nakatomi Plaza, he was dropped a second earlier than he had been told so the crew could film his 'true' reaction!

- Whilst filming *Never Say Never Again*, Sean Connery's wrist was broken by his martial arts instructor. Connery thought nothing of it and only discovered just how bad the injury was years later. His instructor was Steven Seagal.

- To make horses fall over at the right moment during filming, a trip wire called a 'running W' was used for many years. It broke many horses' legs and necks however, and thankfully it is now illegal to use.

- Real machine guns with real bullets were used during the filming of gruelling masterpiece *Come and See*. Actor Aleksey Kravchenko said in one interview that he could hear they bullets as they were travelling through the air just a few centimetres above his head.

- In the iconic scene in 1923's *Safety Last* which was given homage in Back to the Future, Harold Lloyd was in fact hanging from a clock situated twelve stories high... with no safety harness.

- The scene in *The Dark Knight* where the huge truck flips was created without any CGI. Special effects supervisor Chris Corbould actually flipped a life-size truck using a powerful steam piston and a very brave stuntman who was actually driving the vehicle.

- Often considered one of the best movie stunts of all time, in *Raiders of the Lost Ark*, Terry Leonard only agreed to film one scene – where he (as Indiana Jones) crawls along the bottom of a truck which he is then dragged behind with his whip – if fellow stuntman Glenn H Randall Jr was driving the truck. He was particularly cautious because he had attempted a similar stunt earlier on in the year for *Legend of the Lone Ranger,* but the stagecoach used for that scene had actually run over his legs and he was still recovering from the accident!

- The most expensive stunt ever performed was for the film *Cliffhanger*, where stuntman Simon Crane was paid one million dollars to transfer between two jets flying at 15,000 feet.

Cast – Part 2

- Sean Connery has turned down roles in *Blade Runner, Jurassic Park, The Matrix* and *Lord of the Rings*.

- Tom Cruise, John Cusack and Johnny Depp were all considered for the role of Ferris Bueller for his *Day Off*.

- Bill Murray was originally cast as Batman for the 1989 film, however when Tim Burton came on board as director, he immediately reversed the decision.

- Do you know what was the last film the great Orson Wells starred in? It was the cartoon version of *Transformers*, released in 1986. In his last ever interview, when asked what his role was, he couldn't remember which character he played, but said that he was a big toy who attacks a bunch of smaller toys.[1]

- Samuel L Jackson gave permission for the writers of Marvel's *Ultimate* universe to base their version of Nick Fury on him. When the *Avengers* movie was made, it was therefore pretty much a given who would play the part...

- Laurence Fishburne lied about his age to get a part in *Apocalypse Now* – he was just fourteen when he auditioned.,

- Christopher Lee is the only cast or crew member from *Lord of the Rings* to have actually met JRR Tolkien.

---

1. Some suggest Welles's last film was *Someone to Love*, although records show that his scenes for it were shot prior to those from *Transformers*.

- In *Terminator 2,* when the T1000 imitates Sarah Connor, the actress playing the part is actually Linda Hamilton's real-life twin sister, Leslie.

- In her scenes in *Scream*, Drew Barrymore looks incredibly distressed. This wasn't just great acting – director Wes Craven repeatedly told her stories of animal cruelty, which distressed her greatly.

- Despite it being his first ever film, Barkhad Abdi ad-libbed the most famous line in *Captain Phillips*: "Look at me. I'm the captain now".

Going Mad

- According to Stephen King, when filming *The Shining*, director Stanley Kubrick would regularly call him during the middle of the night to ask questions about the story. One particularly amusing call had Kubrick asking King if he believed in God. King replied "Yes", and Kubrick shouted "I knew it!", slamming the phone down.

- Whilst filming *Fight Club*, David Fincher repeatedly re-shot a difficult and painful scene where a stuntman had to fall down some stairs – twelve times in all. For the final edit he used the very first take.

- It is rumoured that James Cameron kept a nail gun on set with him when filming *Avatar* – he would use it to nail cellphones to the wall if they rang on set.

- To what extent is the 'no animals were harmed' phrase seen at the end of a movie true? Well, on the set of *The Shawshank Redemption*, the Humane Society objected to the use of a live maggot when Brooks feeds a crow. Therefore, for the scene the crew had to find a maggot which had died of natural causes.

- Many of the extras you can see in the background of various scenes in *One Flew Over the Cuckoo's Nest* are actually real mental patients.

- To get into character for *My Left Foot*, Daniel Day Lewis refused to get out of his wheelchair, and even demanded to be spoon fed by assistants.

- Heath Ledger locked himself in his hotel room for a month in preparation for his role as the Joker in *The Dark Knight*.

- Hannibal Lecter never blinks during *Silence of the Lambs* – not even once.

- You might think that *Apocalypse Now* is long as it is... but the director shot an amazing 230 hours of raw footage.

- When he was filming *The Wolf of Wall Street*, Jonah Hill snorted so much fake cocaine that he contracted bronchitis!

Movie Lines

- It is Kane's final words on which the entire plot of *Citizen Kane* revolves, however you might notice that there's no-one else in the room when he dies – so how could anyone know what he said?

- In *The Shawshank Redemption*, Morgan Freeman says the line "Maybe it's 'cause I'm Irish". In the original book, Red *is* actually a white Irishman, the line having been written as a wry acknowledgement of the casting change.

- The famous line from *Cool Hand Luke* – 'What we've got here is failure to communicate' – was not actually in the book on which the film was based. Screenwriter Frank Pierson said it came to him from nowhere when he was typing up the script in his Malibu beach house.

- Another surprisingly unscripted line is from *The Shining*, when Jack Torrance pokes his face through the door he has just chopped through with his axe, and says "Heeeere's Johnny!" Jack Nicholson was mimicking a catchphrase from The Johnny Carson show, and just thought it would add an element of madness and menace to an already tense scene.

- When Will Smith is dragging an alien across the desert in Independence Day, he says "And what the hell is that smell?". This was in fact unscripted – the scene was filmed on Utah's salt flats, and an awful stench of dead shrimp was coming from nearby.

- So you know that famous quote in *Apollo 13*: "Houston, we have a problem"? Well, you've got that wrong... The actual line is "Ah, Houston, we've had a problem".

- There are only one thousand words of spoken dialogue in the whole of the film Bambi.

- Out of all main Disney characters, Dumbo has the least spoken lines – none.

- The story that Matt Damon's character tells about his brothers and the barn in *Saving Private Ryan* was totally made up by Damon himself at the shoot – it wasn't in the script at all.

- According to the American Film Institute, the most famous quote in movie history is "Frankly, my dear, I don't give a damn."

Harry Potter

- A number of scenes featuring Rik Mayall as Peeves were shot for the first *Harry Potter* film but never made it into the final cut.

- The prop department had their work cut out for the Gringotts vault scene in *Deathly Hallows Part 2*; they had to make over two hundred thousand coins for it.

- They also did some amazing work on the Goblet of Fire (from the film of the same name). It was over five feet tall, and hand carved from an entire elm tree.

- Initially, the candles used for the great hall scene in the first film were real, suspended from the ceiling by wires (which were to be digitally removed in post-production). However, the flame from each candle would burn through its wire and they would fall onto the actors' heads... so in the end it was decided they would be fully digital.

- When the Diagon Alley set was made, the designers took inspiration from Charles Dickens's novels – most viewers would agree that it has a very Victorian feel to it.

- Every movie used the same beds for scenes in Harry's dorm. Unfortunately, because they were built when the actors were eleven years old, by the time the last few movies came out they always had to curl up on them to stop them falling over the edges!

- When Alfonso Cuaron was confirmed as the director of the third film in the series, he asked the three main stars to write an essay on their characters. Emma Watson (Hermione) wrote a sixteen-page detailed analysis. Daniel Radcliffe (Harry) scribbled a single page of notes. Rupert Grint (Ron) didn't even start it.

- All of the wands created for the films were specially made on site by the props team, and just like in the stories no two were identical.

- Horror writer Stephen King has said that Dolores Umbridge is the greatest villain since Hannibal Lecter. Praise indeed!

- Over two hundred and fifty real animals were used during the filming of the series; the largest was a hippo and the smallest a centipede.

Humorous Facts

- On the set of *Jaws*, George Lucas put his head in the shark's mouth. Laughing, Steven Spielberg closed the prop's jaws. However, the action malfunctioned, and Lucas got stuck.

- During the filming of *The Wizard of Oz*, one of the actors playing a munchkin fell into a toilet and was trapped there for hours until another cast member found him.

- In *North By Northwest*, Cary Grant was older than his on-screen mother, Jessie Royce Landis.

- For his scene in *Ferris Bueller's Day Off*, Charlie Sheen stayed awake for 48 whole hours so he would look particularly wasted. Now make your own jokes.

- Christopher Plummer hated working on *The Sound of Music*. He called it 'The Sound of Mucus', and said that working with Julie Andrews was like 'being hit over the head with a Valentine's card every day'.

- Whilst filming *Who Framed Roger Rabbit*, Charles Fleischer stood off-screen in a rabbit costume to read his lines. When confused studio bosses visited the set, they expressed concern about the 'poor visual effects'.

- In *Anchorman*, the Mexican restaurant that the women from the TV station visit is called 'Escipimos en su Alimento'. This translates as 'We spit in your food'.

- In order to avoid media publicity, *Return of the Jedi* was filmed under the alias *Blue Harvest: Horror Beyond Imagination*.

- We know that films aren't always that realistic, however *Fast & Furious 6* really takes the biscuit. If the runway in the final action scene was real, it would be twenty-six miles long. Even the longest one in the world is only three and a half miles in length.

- Despite the long conversation in *Pulp Fiction*, a quarter pounder with cheese is not known as a royale with cheese anywhere in the world.

More Amazing Facts

- During the filming of *Lord of the Rings*, Christopher Lee corrected Peter Jackson on the sound a man would make if he was stabbed in the back. During WWII, Lee had been an undercover agent for the British Government...

- The sound of the alien spaceship's weapon exploding at the end of *Independence Day* is in fact 'ambassador of soul' James Brown screaming, but put through a number of audio processes.

- The film *Tron* was banned from the category of 'best special effects' at that year's Oscars. The judging panel felt that using a computer for special effects was cheating.

- Ridley Scott was the fifth choice director for *Alien* – he only got the gig as those above him in the pecking order were working on other projects or declined the opportunity.

- Movies involving time travel are banned in China.

- The first movie ever broadcast on television was *The Crooked Circle* in 1933. It was still being played in cinemas at the time, yet the filmmakers thought it would be excellent publicity. Nowadays of course, there is a usually a contractual minimum amount of time before a broadcast version is permitted.

- Having quit college 33 years earlier to focus on his movie career, Steven Spielberg went back to finish his course in 2002. He turned in *Schindler's List* as his student film.

- Because he was a relatively unknown author at the time, the trailer for *Carrie* incorrectly spells Stephen King's first name as 'Steven'.

- On the set of *Armageddon*, Ben Affleck asked director Michael Bay why NASA would send an inexperienced drill crew into space when it would be much easier to teach astronauts how to drill. Bay told him to shut up.

- The director of *Cannibal Holocaust* actually had to prove in court that the actors weren't killed during the filming of the movie – as people at the time thought it was too realistic.

And Finally...

- During his presidential campaign, hopeful candidate Herman Cain quoted a 'famous poet', saying "Life can be a challenge, life can seem impossible. It's never easy when there's so much on the line. But you and I can make a difference". It turns out that the quote was in fact from the first *Pokémon* movie.

CPSIA information can be obtained
at www.ICGtesting.com
Printed in the USA
LVHW101020310322
714896LV00033B/241

9 781785 381300